52 Simple Ways
ᴛᴏ Start a
GARDEN

How to Be Sustainable, Save Money,
and Eat Homegrown Food

Terri Paajanen

FIG

Terri Paajanen/Mango Media, Inc.
2525 Ponce de Leon, Suite 300
Coral Gables, FL 33134
www.mangomedia.us

52 Simple Ways to Garden / Terri Paajanen-- 1st ed.
ISBN 978-1-63353-075-1

"My garden is my most beautiful masterpiece."
— Claude Monet

Contents

Level ①

Digging In

Take Lots of Notes

With so many variables in the garden,
don't expect everything to run precisely
like clockwork from one year to the next.

Take Lots of Notes

This is one tip you'll want to start on right from the beginning, even if you don't feel like you have any idea what you're doing yet. Keep track of everything you do so you can refer back to it in future years.

The main things to record are:

- Dates you plant and harvest
- Any unusual weather
- When you added fertilizer or pesticide
- Which sprays did or did not work

But it's the planting dates you want to remember most of all. Focus on that to start with. If you plant your spring peas too late, then they won't be done in time to plant that patch with more summer vegetables. If you get your peppers started too late, they may not be ready to harvest before that first frost. What works (or doesn't work) for you one year can help guide you the next.

Keep track of harvesting too.

Knowing when that big rush of green beans is about to start can be a good heads-up to get your kitchen ready for a big canning session.

Take note of the elements.

Knowing that you have to be ready with the insect sprays by the second week of June in order to protect your tomatoes will keep you on track and your precious plants protected. The same goes for unseasonal weather—extra rain, for example. Expect the unexpected.

Get a spiral notebook or start a simple computer spreadsheet. How you organize your notes is up to you as long as you do it, but keep them consistent. Paper notebooks are a little sturdier and can be stored out in the garden shed where you're more likely to make notes. Pencil won't run in case your notes get wet, which is a pretty good probability at some point. On the other hand, a digital file can make it easier to go searching for something in several years' worth of text and dates.

Know Your Zone

If you don't already know it, you need to find out what growing zone you're in. That single piece of information will be key in figuring out what plants will grow well based on your local climate. People can make a lot of inaccurate assumptions about what will grow in their area and that can mean you miss out on all kinds of delicious fresh produce.

The zones start in the cold north, and the numbers increase as you move southward. Technically, the scale runs from 1 to 20, but most people will find themselves between 4 and 10. The zone designations tend to create bands as you move north to south, but being on the coast or near other features like lakes or mountains will affect your zone.

Once you know your zone, look for it on the seeds you buy to see what will grow for you. Labelling tends to be a certain zone "and up" because plants usually have a cold tolerance level you can't drop below, but the upper heat tolerance is not as important.

Check out some seeds you may not have thought suitable for your area, you might be surprised. Even within one family of plants, there can be variations that are better for one zone over another. Cool-weather varieties may exist that can broaden your choices. Knowing your zone is the first step.

You can take a few chances too. A plant that is fine for Zone 5 and up may still work in your Zone 4 home if you take a little extra care with plant covers and extra mulch layers. But hoping that a tropical Zone 7 will thrive in the cold is not too realistic.

Know Your Zone

You can find graphic zone maps around on the Internet, but the **USDA website is a good place to start.**

TIP

Oddly enough, **some plants get better after a light frost.**
Kale will get sweeter if the leaves get a frosting
before you harvest, for example.

Watch Your Frost Dates

Unless you are enjoying life in a tropical paradise, most people have to watch out for the frosts of winter every year. For many plants, frost is a killer and you should be planning out your entire season around the 2 frost dates. The dates are based on historical averages, so don't consider them 100% guaranteed by any means.

First, there is the date of last frost in the spring. Many folks consider this the starting point for the growing season even though many plants can be planted (or started indoors) before this date. Once the threat of frost is passed, anything can be planted outside safely.

Then you have your first frost date in late fall, roughly marking the end of your growing season. You should keep a close eye on this one, but it's the immediate forecast that matters. If you have some end-of-the-season plants still out in the garden, and they're calling for freezing temperatures, then you'll want to get things picked and harvested right away. On the other hand, if the date has arrived and the forecast is still warm and balmy, just enjoy it and let your plants have a few more days to grow.

If you have vulnerable plants out there and an unexpected frost is predicted, don't despair. A light covering of cloth or plastic can do wonders in protecting your plants if you don't have time to get out there and pick. Also, a frost can be followed by a week or more of frost-free weather. It would be a shame to yank all your plants before necessary.

You can find out your local frost dates by checking with the extension office for your area, or finding a website online with maps.

Why is frost such a problem? Once the temperature drops below freezing at night, the water will freeze in the tissues of your plants. Ice crystals form which then burst the little plant cells, causing all kinds of damage. Some plants can withstand a little frost, some will turn to dead green mush after one single frosty night. Get to know which of your plants handle frost so you don't panic in the cold.

Start with Herbs

With the list of potential fruits and vegetables for your garden being so long, it can be daunting to know where to begin. What's the best place to start for the ultimate gardening novice? Herbs can be the answer. They tend to be very low maintenance, take up little space and will give you an easy harvest of aromatic leaves.

You can grow many herbs indoors in containers, or get an outdoor garden started. Many kitchen herbs are perennials so if you do start growing outside, plan ahead because your plants can be in that spot for many years to come.

A few you might consider trying:

Basil: A staple in many kitchens, it grows very well as long as it gets plenty of sunshine. It's great for flavoring or making home-made pesto.

Oregano: Another good cooking herb, especially if you love Italian cuisine. Like the basil, give your plants lots of sun.

Mint: Mint will grow like a weed, and spread farther than you'd like if you're not careful it's ideal for a large pot. You can use the leaves in cooking, baking or to make tea. Partial shade is best for mint plants.

Lemon balm: You can make some excellent zesty lemon tea with lemon balm leaves, and it grows easily in sun or partial shade. Just pinch out any developing flowers to keep your plant leafy.

Dill: Dill will grow with almost no attention from you whatsoever. It's a fairly tall plant and best left to outdoor growing though. You can harvest the fine leaves or wait for the seed at the end of the season. It needs full sun and can shade other plants nearby.

Chamomile: This is one herb you are harvesting flowers from rather than leaves. They like lots of sun, and you can pick the pretty white flowers to dry for tea later in the summer.

Besides how easy herbs are to grow, the strong scents are good at naturally keeping away the bugs. You'll have few insect pests to deal with in most herb gardens, which means one less headache as you build up your gardening skills.

Start with Herbs

TIP

In the fall, **cover your herbs with a layer of mulch** if they are outside, and they should be fine to **perk back up on their own come spring.**

Perennials vs. Annuals

Not only does a **perennial take up more room** after a while, it starts to get **less productive as the clump grows.**

Perennials vs. Annuals

Just a little terminology tip, so you understand better about the kinds of plants you are growing and how they will grow from year to year. For most gardens, you'll be dealing with either annuals or perennials.

Annuals: These are plants that just live one year, produce seed and die. Almost all typical garden vegetables fall into this category, like cucumbers, tomatoes, beans, lettuce, peppers or pumpkins. Some herbs are also annuals, such as basil or chamomile.

One quirk about some annuals, like chamomile for example, is that they reseed themselves so readily that they seem to come up every year like a perennial. In most vegetable cases, you'll be harvesting seeds or fruit, so this kind of self-seeding doesn't happen.

Perennials: Now these are the plants that stay living over the winter, even though their above-ground portions die back, and then naturally re-sprout come spring. Chives, sage and lavender are common herbal perennials. You won't find too many vegetables that are, though. Asparagus and rhubarb are two that will come up again and again for you. Fruits are usually perennials, so strawberries, blueberries and raspberries fall into this category.

Though the idea of plants that don't need replanting each spring is appealing, there is a wee downside to perennials. As each plant continues to grow, year after year, it gets larger. Eventually, it will outgrow its allotted space and require pruning, splitting or other kinds of maintenance.

Biennial: We don't hear about biennial plants all that often, though it's not as rare as you might think. These are plants that will grow for 2 years before flowering and dying. We usually harvest these vegetables after their first year, so the second year doesn't matter that much, unless you are planning on saving seeds. Carrots, cauliflower, turnip, chard and Brussels sprouts are biennials, though most people don't even realize it.

North vs. South

You don't need to be a Civil War buff to understand the nature of the north vs. south conflict in your garden. It's all about sunshine and how to get the most of it.

Unless you live at the equator, the sun will always be on the southern side of the sky as it moves from east to west (though if you are in the southern hemisphere, everything in this tip is opposite). So look to the south for the most sunlight.

For a yard that is relatively flat, the worry about north or south doesn't mean much. Your garden isn't "facing" any direction to begin with. It does make a difference when you have trees or buildings around your space. If your garden is on the north side of the house, it will be shaded a lot more than if it were on the south side.

All of this also applies to indoor gardening, even more so because that window is the only source of light for your plants. Get your plants in south-facing windows as often as you can, unless they are cool-weather plants that prefer much less sun.

The issues with sunlight in east vs. west is also worth considering though the sun moves from one side to the other over the day. That means that any shade you get in the morning will be in full sun by evening.

Don't worry if all this direction talk gets you turned around. For the most part, your garden will do just fine. As we said, a typical level garden doesn't really "face" anywhere. It's about taking note of the sun's position and getting things oriented for the best results.

North vs. South

Look for slight hills or dips in your land as well, **keep your plants on the south-facing side** as much as you can to eliminate as much shade as you can.

Windowsill Gardening

If you're determined to have a **good crop inside,** you might want a few extra lights to supplement your sun.

Windowsill Gardening

Pining for a sunny yard to get your garden going? If you have windows, then you can start working out your green thumb with indoor container gardening.

There are a few important benefits to growing some plants indoors. The main one is that your garden is almost completely protected against pests and bad weather. It can also be a lot nicer to do your chores inside, rather than out in the hot sun.

Ideally, you should have your plants in south-facing windows to get the most light you can. Plants that prefer shade will do fine in any window, or even on a table in the middle of the room. Light that comes in through window glass gets magnified, so a plant can get very hot even though it's indoors. Not all plants need so much heat, so use a small thermometer in your growing areas. If it gets far hotter than outside temperatures would be, you need to block the sun slightly or move your plants a little farther from the window.

Water when the soil is dry to the touch, and make sure you use containers that have good drainage and a tray underneath them. A shot of natural fertilizer or compost a few times throughout the season will keep the nutrients up.

The best plants for gardening in the window are herbs and other leafy vegetables. Basil, mint and thyme will all do very well in any sunny spot. A pot or two of lettuce would give you fresh greens too.

You can try out some larger vegetables, but choose smaller plants whenever possible, particularly dwarf or mini versions. Not only do they take up less space, they will require less light and energy to produce for you. Cherry tomatoes and miniature cucumbers are a couple of great examples.

Do a little research on pollination too. Without the usual host of flies and bees, your plants will not naturally be pollinated, which will mean no fruit. As long as you grow more than one plant, you can do the job yourself with a light paintbrush.

Gardening Toolbox

You shouldn't need a huge shed full of tools to keep your garden going, even though the latest gadgets can be tempting. To get started, you'll want to have the basics.

Spade & Hand Trowel: A good shovel can be your best friend. In the spring, it is a vital tool to turn over soil and remove manure. A hand trowel is better for smaller jobs, like transplanting seedlings.

Rake: For smoothing out soil, spreading mulch or gathering up debris around the garden.

Watering Cans: Even if you plan on using a hose to water with, a good watering can (or two) can be helpful for spot treatments and for when you don't want to drag a length of hose along behind you.

Buckets: A collection of various size buckets will never go amiss in a garden. From hauling water, seedlings, compost, other tools or collecting newly picked vegetables, they will always be in demand.

Hoe: A hoe is ideal for breaking up clumps of soil and hacking down emerging little weedlings.

Spray bottles: Plastic bottles with a trigger spray will come in handy so many times. When you mix up your own insect sprays, you'll need some way to apply them.

Pruning shears: These are good for trimming stems, cutting off dead leaves or to harvest your vegetables with. Scissors aren't going to cut it.

Gloves: Get a sturdy pair of leather gloves that fit you well. Invest in good quality or you'll end up buying new gloves every year.

Gardening Toolbox

TIP

If you've got the budget and a place to store it, then a wheelbarrow **will make** some of **your chores a whole lot easier.**

Get a Water Barrel

Get a Water Barrel

Some people are blessed with a local climate that brings regular rainfall all summer long and they never have to concern themselves with watering chores. Most gardeners aren't that lucky. To save yourself the hit to your water bill, try to get one or more water barrels working for you.

They are getting to be a common sight around household gardens, especially in the city. You can probably get barrels at any large garden store but you can go with a more DIY approach if you can find access to empty barrels that only had food-grade materials in them before they were emptied. With a commercial barrel, you'll likely get a screened lid and a spigot you can attach a hose to. Both are very useful features.

For a salvaged barrel, you should make a screened lid of your own to keep out egg-laying mosquitoes as well as grass cuttings and loose leaves. Too much debris can really muck up your water.

A typical barrel will be around 50 gallons, and if you have a good-sized roof collecting water, you can actually fill that volume with just one good rain storm. A 40x40 section of flat roof will collect 2 full barrels after just 1 inch of rainfall. If you have space, two or three will really create a good water supply for you. That can mean thousands of gallons of free water for your garden.

Not only does a water barrel system allow you to have an environmentally-friendly water source on hand, the water is actually better for your plants than city tap water. Rain water is free of any chlorine or fluoride treatments, and it will be naturally soft (i.e. free of dissolved minerals that can be a problem with household water).

TIP

Have your barrel set out at the end of your downspout, and you'll **start collecting** your own **free water** the next time it rains.

Watering the Right Way

Though Mother Nature's way of watering already does a pretty good job of keeping your fruits and vegetables healthy and thriving, there are a few little tips you can pick up to make your manual watering more effective for your garden.

When watering your plants, you want to keep the water down at the soil level as much as possible. Waving a hose over all your plants is going to soak the leaves and potentially leave your soil dry.

Not only does it mean your plants' roots aren't getting the water they need, you're creating a damp atmosphere among all your foliage. Yes, that's what happens when it rains anyway, but there is no need to make it worse on purpose. Wet leaves can lead to mildew, and you don't want that. Soaking the leaves also washes away any insecticide treatments you may have used, meaning you'll just have to go out and reapply later.

Point your hose nozzle low and near the ground if you can, or get one of those handy long attachments to help save your back. When watering by hand, get a watering can with a long spout for the same reason. Get under the leaves and pour directly to the soil.

Rain water is the best for your plants, so a water barrel or two can help you keep a supply of that on hand. Rural tap water is also fine but if you have a chlorinated municipal water supply, then you might want to take an extra step to keep the chemicals out of your soil.

With a large garden, this may not be practical though and that would be OK too. It's a step you can take as long as it works for you.

TIP

Fill up your water cans or buckets with tap water, **then let them sit out overnight.** Most of the chlorine will naturally evaporate out by then, and **you can get watering with cleaner water.**

Watering the Right Way

Mulch

For seedlings, add your mulch around them giving
several inches of open space
so you don't accidentally harm the little plants.
As they grow, shift the mulch
in closer until your layer is right around your plant stems.

Mulch

For the beginning gardener, this is one of the first techniques you should embrace no matter how big or small your garden is. Mulch does lots of great stuff for your plants, and it actually makes your gardening chores easier.

Firstly, a good layer of mulch holds in a lot of moisture. Nice damp soil means healthier plants and less time spent watering for you. This can be particularly vital during those hot summer months when it never seems to rain enough. And don't worry, as long as the mulch is loose enough, water easily flows through it all to get to the soil. You're not blocking the water by mulching.

And if that wasn't enough, you can get a second major benefit from your mulch. If the layer is thick, you'll also be blocking out all the weeds. In areas where water isn't a problem, this can still make mulching worthwhile. You'll need to be diligent though. Any thin spots in your layer and those stubborn weeds will take advantage of it.

What to Use: You don't need to have any special mulching materials. It just needs to be natural, loose and porous. The usual ingredients are straw, wood chips or even old newspapers. Straw and chips work best. Newspapers can create too tight a layer, and can block incoming water more than you want. Tear them up and keep it fluffy to make good mulch.

You can buy porous fabric that will work fine for mulching, just check at your local garden center. Depending on the shape of the material, you might need to cut small holes for the plants to grow through. The investment may be worth it as you can usually reuse the fabric over a few years.

The Technique: The trick is to get a thick enough layer of mulch. It packs down after a few rains, and can spread out by animals. You'll want at least 6 inches of material, though you can build up to that over the course of several applications, especially if you are starting with very small seedlings. Don't smother tiny plants! Thin mulch layers will still help with water retention, but the weeds will happily grow right on through it.

Start Composting

Y ou may already be doing this as a way to cut down on your kitchen garbage. But if you don't already have a compost bin or pile going, you're going to want to start.

Quick List of Compostable Items

There is more to compost than just grass clippings and apple cores. These are the kinds of things you want to add to your compost as often as you can:

- All fruit and vegetable scraps (peels, leaves, seeds, cores, etc.)
- Stale bread and crusts
- Leftover pasta (cooked or not)
- Coffee grounds
- Egg shells
- Used tea bags (as long as they're not the silk kind)
- Yard waste
- Occasional used paper towels or tissue

Leave out: meat scraps, oily or greasy foods, anything toxic or non-degradable.

Get Composting: Once you start collecting your organic materials, you'll need a place to put them. The easiest approach is to just set a spot aside and start piling. It may not look great but it's easy, and does allow better access for turning and harvesting your finished fertilizer. You do run the risk of animals rooting around through your scraps though. A large bin (like a big garbage can, or larger) should have a lid and several holes to allow for aeration. Your compost will dry out faster this way, compared to the pile. It's up to you which approach to take.

Dump your scraps and material as you accumulate it. A mix of "dry" stuff like grass clippings or shredded newspaper need to be balanced by "wet" stuff like kitchen food scraps. Too much of either and it won't turn into compost. During hot weather, add some water to keep it all moist. Insects, worms and fungus need a damp environment to do their work.

Periodically, give it a stir or a turn-over with a shovel. After about a season, there should be a deep black layer of crumbly compost at the bottom of your bin. It's ready to be mixed in with your garden soil at this point.

Start Composting

No Space?

If you live in an apartment or any home with no yard space, you don't have to give up your composting dreams. Try your hand at vermicomposting (that's composting with worms). Having your own population of worms in the compost bin means your compost breaks down a lot faster than in an outside bin. And it's not as gross as it might sound.

A large plastic container (like a storage tote) is all you need. Drill some holes in the lid for air, and you have a worm home. Keep the container about half full of damp shredded newspapers and add worms (check the garden store). Add your daily contributions of scraps. The worms eat your waste as well as the newspapers, leaving you with handfuls of black "castings" (the nice name for worm poop). This is excellent fertilizer for your plants.

TIP

Decomposed organic scraps become rich fertilizer that will really give your plants a nutrient boost. It's a natural and *FREE* option.

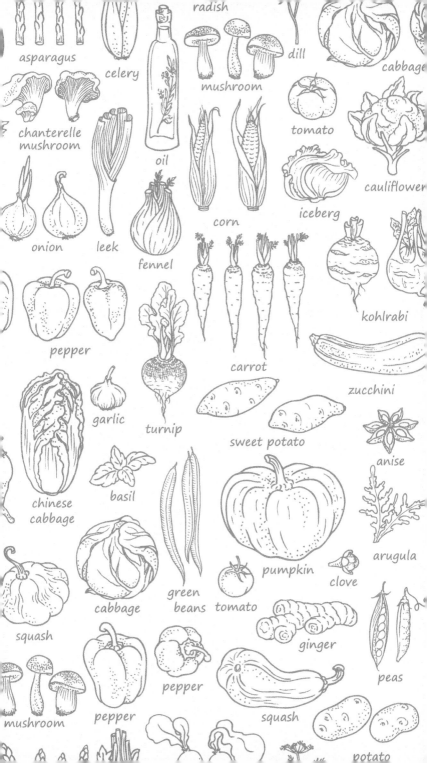

asparagus

celery

radish

mushroom

dill

cabbage

chanterelle
mushroom

oil

tomato

cauliflower

onion

leek

fennel

corn

iceberg

pepper

carrot

kohlrabi

turnip

sweet potato

zucchini

garlic

anise

chinese
cabbage

basil

arugula

pumpkin

clove

squash

cabbage

green
beans

tomato

ginger

peas

mushroom

pepper

pepper

squash

potato

Grow What You Eat

TIP

Don't grow anything just because you can.
It's a waste of time *AND* valuable resources.

Grow What You Eat

This is a tip to help you change your mindset, rather than a new gardening technique to try. Overall, it will bring a more satisfying gardening experience and less wasted food.

Grow what you eat and eat what you grow.

Remember this little mantra next spring when you're getting your seeds ready.

The point is that you should only grow what your family will actually eat, and once you do harvest it, it gets used up. Don't keep growing things out of habit or convention if they're not really needed (or wanted).

Growing tomatoes is a common tradition for most people in North America. It's just one of those vegetables that "everybody" has in their gardens. But what if you never use tomatoes? Then don't bother growing them. The opposite applies, too. If you get an enormous bumper crop of snap peas this year, that's what you eat—even if it's for weeks on end.

It will likely take a few years to really work out what your family needs and wants, particularly when it comes to the amount of food you produce. If one long row of black beans isn't enough, go for 2 next year. This is all part of your annual note-taking chore. Eventually, you can fine-tune your garden space to suit your family's personal palate.

Thin Out the Seedlings

This can be a painful chore, but it's a necessary one that you really can't ignore. As your precious seeds germinate and sprout, you will have to remove any extras or any little plants that are too close to each other.

Once you've planted out your seeds in the spring, it's always a real thrill to see all those little green shoots after a week or so. You will hate to yank them up. It's important, so do it anyway. Just make sure you're doing it right.

First of all, know what spacing you're after. Use the seed packets as a guide for this. Your plants may not need as much space as you think, and you wouldn't want to over-pluck your seedlings. It might seem logical to you to allow less space than recommended because more plants means more food. Though two stunted plants might produce more food than 1 healthy one, you will also run the risk of mildew and insect infestation when plants are too clustered together.

Don't start thinning too soon. Pulling up shoots after only letting them grow for two days isn't the right approach. Give the plants you're leaving time to get their roots in place, so you don't end up pulling or damaging them. Slow-growing plants like carrot can wait several weeks before you need to thin. You also want to make sure that the plants you're leaving are truly thriving and doing fine. Also, with a little growth under their belts, those pulled thinning can actually be put to use.

Many greens can be used even as tiny sprouts, and larger vegetables like broccoli, cabbage or beets have edible greens at first too. So collect everything when you are thinning, wash them up and add them to dinner. Food is food, after all.

Technically, you could avoid the need to thin by being super meticulous when you place every seed, and allow the proper spacing right from day one. This isn't a really good approach. Several of your seeds are sure to not germinate, which will leave you with lots of wasted empty space. Overplanting and then thinning really is the best approach.

Thin Out the Seedlings

TIP

If you find later that you didn't thin enough the mature plants are getting crowded, don't thin them. You'll do too much damage to the roots of the remaining plants at this point.

Get to Know the Good Bugs

TIP

If you don't recognize some of these insects, **a quick search online should bring up some good photos** OR you might want an identification guide for your book collection.

Get to Know the Good Bugs

B efore you go too crazy with the insect sprays, you should get a little familiar with your local bug population so you can tell which ones are problematic. Many common insects are actually very helpful in the garden and should be considered your allies, not enemies.

Bees: This is no surprise as most gardeners know that these buzzing bugs are the main force behind the pollination of your plants. Unlike wasps or hornets, bees pose little threat for stinging as long as you leave them alone.

Ladybugs: These bright red and black beetles do not harm your plants whatsoever, and are known to eat aphids (who do harm your plants). The adult beetles aren't the big bonus, it's their squat black and orange larvae that are the real heroes. They're so awesome that big garden stores even sell boxes of live ladybugs just in case you want more of them.

Lacewings: Lacewings are delicate-looking green flies with large wings. Again, it's mainly their larvae you want to have around, so leave the adults alone when you see them and hope they lay some eggs. They eat a bunch of smaller insects like aphids, thrips, scale, small caterpillars and more.

Ground Beetles: A little harder to identify, but these black beetles live in the soil and can help take care of slugs, maggots and cutworms.

Assassin bugs and Damsel bugs: These two species look similar and once you know what they look like, you'll know to leave them be. They eat a lot of destructive bugs, and they'll give you a sharp bite if you try to pick them up.

Spiders: Technically these guys attack the bad bugs as well as other good bugs, but overall they do a fine job of insect pest control. It's so tempting to kill them because they give people the creeps. Toughen up and let them do their job in the garden.

Natural Pesticides

Trying to keep your garden all-natural and organic in the face of relentless attacks can make you crazy. After losing another batch of plants to hungry bugs, anyone would want to grab the nearest spray bottle of something toxic. Thankfully, there are a few really good pesticide options that aren't horrendous for the Earth or for you.

The Finger Treatment: This is as natural and old-school as you can get. Just pick the offending bugs off, and drop them in a bucket with a little soapy water. It's ideal for larger caterpillars or beetles that are easy to see and grab. Tiny aphids will need another approach.

Diatomaceous Earth (DE): Diatomaceous earth is a fine white powder you can buy at the garden store, and it's completely harmless to people, plants and animals. On a microscopic scale, it has lots of sharp edges from teeny broken seashells. It feels like baking soda to you or me, but will be like glass shards to a bug. Just sprinkle it around your plants, and the pests are dead almost on contact with it.

Soap Spray: Mix 5 tablespoons of pure liquid soap with a gallon of water. Shake it up in a spray bottle and give a spritz when you see small bugs on your plants. For a more powerful variation on this recipe, add a teaspoon of hot red pepper powder to about a gallon of spray. That will really keep the larger bugs away.

Essential Oils: A strongly scented essential oil can repel insects without doing them any actual harm. A mixture of roughly 4oz water, 4 oz. witch hazel and 30+ drops of a potent oil-like clove, cinnamon, mint, rosemary or eucalyptus will work in a spray bottle. Shake well, and spritz your plants to start driving away the bugs.

Pyrethrum Sprays: Look for commercial products with pyrethrum for a potent and relatively safe insect repellent. It is a toxin (just a very mild and natural one), so take care when using. It will kill most insects and it lingers on the plants, so spraying the leaves will help keep the insects off until it rains. Unlike the soap, you don't actually have to dose the pests directly.

Natural Pesticides

A combination of several of these techniques should be enough to keep pests away **without having to resort to anything** really **unhealthy for your plants.**

Level ②

Gone to Seed

Starting Seeds Indoors

TIP

For indoor sprouting, a fluorescent light is nice 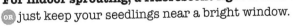 OR just keep your seedlings near a bright window.

Starting Seeds Indoors

You can give your plants a healthy head-start by starting your seeds inside, providing you have the space. Don't worry, you don't have to set up racks of grow lights to make this work either.

Seeds are usually planted out based on the temperature outside. Some seeds can tolerate colder weather, and they can be planted in spring, some prefer more heat and wait until later. They don't really care about the time or date, just how warm it is. That means you can get a leg up on the season inside. You still need to wait for their appropriate temperature outside to plant in the garden though.

For plants that need to go out 2 weeks after the last frost, you can start seeds 2 weeks before the frost date. That means you have month-old seedlings at planting time instead of just getting your seeds into the ground that day. If you have a shorter growing season to start with, that'll make a huge difference.

Just don't overdo it. You don't want to be dealing with seedlings that are too old at transplant time. They are more likely to be damaged during the move and the shift in light and climate can be pretty shocking to their systems. Each plant is unique in this, so check the seed packages. Overall, a few weeks are fine and some sun-loving plants can even be started 6 to 8 weeks before they go outside.

Planting seeds inside is just like doing it out in the garden. Some need to be on the soil surface, some just covered, and some will need to be an inch or more down. It matters, so read your seed packs. Start them off in those standard little compartment trays or use small recycled containers (like yogurt cups).

Use a good quality potting soil, mixed with a little loose compost for the best results. Older plants can tolerate a little dry soil, but not your germinating seeds. Keep the soil slightly damp at all times. Light isn't that important at first, it's the moisture that gets your seeds going. Once they've sprouted, there needs to be good light through the day.

Even if you don't want to have your plants in the house for weeks on end, even just a few days to get the seeds germinated can provide some help for your new plants.

Apartment Gardening

A re you excited to grow your own food, but literally haven't got a square inch of soil to your name? Have no fear! You can actually raise a number of plants in an apartment to still have a tasty harvest of your own.

Indoor Containers: With a sunny window, you can grow all sorts of herbs and leafy greens indoors for a year-round gardening experience. Smaller vegetables will also work, though you'll have to experiment a bit to see what will produce for you. Little cherry tomatoes, miniature cucumbers or peppers can all grow fine. Perhaps even a small strawberry plant. The sections on container and windowsill gardening have more tips for this.

If your sunlight situation isn't ideal, try a few extra lights. They don't have to be fancy or expensive grow-lights, just a standard fluorescent light will do. Have it on a timer to give your plants around 14 hours of light for the best results.

You'll have much fewer pests to deal with indoors, so you actually have a bit of an advantage over outdoor gardening that way. Keep your potted plants nicely watered, and that's all there is to it.

Using the Balcony: If you don't have a balcony, you will have to make do with just the indoor pots. But if you do have one, you can get loads of plants growing out in that little outdoor oasis. You'll get natural sunlight and rainwater, as well as some additional space. Watch the water though. If your balcony has another one directly overhead, your plants may not get the soaking you think during a rain. And speaking of water, be courteous when watering. Run-off from your pots can end up dripping all over the balcony below you. You don't want anyone complaining about your garden to the landlord.

One unique obstacle for urban apartment gardening is pollution. Balconies that look out over busy streets are fine for people-watching, but may be a poor spot to grow healthy food. The fumes from the cars below are most certainly going to end up being absorbed by your plants. In that case, you're going to be better passing on that sunshine and sticking to indoor plants only.

Apartment Gardening

Make the most of every square inch
by training plants to grow upward as much as possible.

PLANTS

Container Gardening

Container Gardening

This is a tip that applies to anyone but it will be most appropriate for all the gardeners who are trying to garden without much yard space. Pots and containers can be used for much more than just a few patio geraniums.

Just about any plant can grow in a container, even a small tree, as long as the container is big enough. You can also maximize your available pot space by choosing smaller varieties of plants to begin with. Many vegetables and even fruit can come in "dwarf" varieties that are better suited to container conditions. A little bush of cherry tomatoes can give you a big harvest, and it will work better in a pot than a huge sprawling vine of beefsteaks.

You can "layer" your garden better with pots too. Add some tables, shelves or hanging pots to boost your available space. Just take care not to create too much shade for the other plants this way.

Not only does a container allow you to add more growing space to a small area (even an apartment balcony), there are other benefits to container gardening too. Pots are portable, so you can control sun and rain exposure when you need to by shifting their position as the seasons change. Plants in containers are also more protected from soil-travelling insect pests or burrowing rodents. You'll also have a bit better control over fertilizing and watering, and plants that spread too easily will be more contained.

But speaking of watering, potted plants will dry out faster, so there can be some additional watering chores if the rain isn't taking care of that.

Fill with a good quality soil, adding some small stones to the bottom to help with drainage (and to keep the soil from dribbling out the holes). Trays underneath are a good way to hold on to a bit of extra water, but aren't crucial to keeping your plants in containers.

It can be a little tougher to add compost and natural fertilizer to a potted plant because you have less space to work with. At the start of the growing season, mix a handful into the soil and then add a little more to the top of the container as the plant grows. Just soak your compost for a few days, strain out the solids and use the water. Voila, homemade liquid fertilizer.

Vertical Gardening

Like container gardening, this is the kind of tip you need when you're trying to do your gardening in a small space. Using your vertical space can make a huge difference in how much room you really need to get a big harvest from your plants.

First, going vertical brings the plants up to your level to make many other chores easier on your back. Clipping back dead leaves, treating insect pests, and harvesting are all easier to manage when they are up off the ground and closer to eye level. Having your plants up in the air adds more ventilation and that can help reduce any mold or mildew that plagues plants that are normally clustered together or low to the ground. Same goes for any fruit that would normally sit on the soil while it's ripening. On that note, having your fruit in the air will also protect against some soil-bound pests like slugs.

Another thing to consider is the difference between a vining variety and a bush variety for many plants. When you choose a bush variety, you get a more compact plant but you typically get a smaller harvest in the end. A vining type usually produces a much larger (and sprawling) plant and more vegetables for you.

The Techniques: First of all, you need to understand that not all vining plants will naturally twist themselves up your trellis supports. Pole beans and peas will happily grow like little corkscrews around whatever they come in contact with, but tomatoes or cucumbers will not. In these cases, you'll need to gently position the growing branches of the plants against your supports, and tie them in place. Rough string may rub and cut into the tender stems of your plants. You'll have to be more strategic on where you place your plants because high trellises loaded with vines will create a lot of shade for any other garden beds nearby.

To build a trellis, you can get creative with any kinds of poles, straight branches or even plumbing piping. Your plants may be tied directly to the poles, or you can hang twine to give them an easier gripping surface. How high? That depends on your plant. It's fairly common for vining plants to reach 7 or 8 feet, so don't skimp on your supports. For plants that only get to 3 or 4 feet high, a piece of chicken wire fencing can make an excellent support.

Vertical Gardening

Whatever you use, make it sturdy.

Once you have your plants growing *AND* producing at full tilt, **they will create a lot of weight on your supports.**

The Art of Transplanting

The Art of Transplanting

For any seeds that you start inside, eventually you'll need to transplant them out into the garden (unless you're doing indoor container gardening of course). Once the right time has come to get your seedlings outside, usually after your spring frost date, know the right way to safely get your plants moved to their outdoor locations.

Hardening Off: Seedlings that have lived a coddled life inside your house can get a bit of a shock when suddenly outside. Lighting and temperatures changes are significant, and a tender indoor seedling hasn't toughened up to withstand the normal breezes you get outside.

Let them ease into the change by exposing them to the outside gradually, a technique called "hardening off." If you have a large number of seedlings, it can be a difficult task, so don't feel it is crucially necessary. Otherwise, place your seedling trays outside on warm days for a week or two before actually planting out.

The Move: First start off by digging some holes, large enough to hold each seedling and the soil that will be coming along with them. Add a little compost to the hole so your new plants get a nutrient boost right from the start.

Ease the seedling out of its pot, ideally holding the dirt in place around the roots. Firmly set into its hole, and add loose soil to support it. After your plants are in place, give them a gentle watering and keep the soil moist until they are well-established and thriving.

Skip the Whole Thing: Some plants really shouldn't be transplanted at all. Their seed packets will usually specify that they should only be planted directly out into the garden. Usually it's because their roots are fragile and just don't tolerate being moved. Heed the warning and just plant them in the garden when the time is right, or you run the serious risk of killing your little plants when you move them.

Testing Your Soil

You don't need to be a chemist to start understanding the nutrients in your soil, and it can make a huge difference in your plant's health to know what's going on in your dirt.

Soil testing kits are easy to find at any gardening store, and they are very easy to use. There are two basic types: the dip strip and the tablet test. They both rely on colors to show you the amount of any given nutrient or mineral in your soil.

Basically, you just take a sample of your soil and add it to water. Then either add a tablet to the water or dip the test strip into the water. When the color changes, you compare it to the little chart provided in the kit. The darker the colors, the higher nutrient levels you have.

Test at least for nitrogen, potassium, phosphorus, and pH level (the acidity of your soil).Once you know what your soil is lacking, you can figure out the best fertilizers to get it into shape.

Chemical content isn't the only thing you'll want to be testing for. Soil drainage is pretty important too. Generally most plants like a loose soil that drains well. If your garden has clay-laden soil that is thick and holds on to water, your plants' roots will soon suffer as they struggle for air. Best to check on the drainage before planting.

The usual way is to dig a 1-foot deep hole and fill it with water. Once it drains out completely, fill it up again. Now measure the water level in inches. Give it 15 minutes, then measure again. When you see how much it's dropped, multiply that by 4 to see how many inches per hour. You want to see 1 to 6 inches per hour for most plants. Less than that, and you need to mix in loose compost, sand or wood shavings to help keep the water moving.

Testing Your Soil

These tests aren't just a one-time thing you do when you first start gardening. After a few years of crops, **your soil will likely start to change.**

Support Your Plants

Support Your Plants

One of the minor downsides of a wonderfully thriving garden is that the plants can really start to get big. And the bigger they get, the more support they are going to need.

Sprawling Vine Types: If you are growing things like cucumbers, beans, tomatoes or melons that are a vining variety, you have a bit more flexibility on what to do.

Vining plants can grow 7 or 8 feet high (or taller), so plan your trellis with some good height on it. Three poles tied at the top with wire make an easy tripod-style of trellis. Vines can either grow naturally up the poles, or you can use soft twine or wire to fasten your plants to the poles.

Compact Bush Types: Plants that are designed to grow in a bush form are usually better at holding themselves up, but are also more likely to get snapped branches if they are too heavily laden with fruit. Unlike vines, they're not quite as flexible and not really meant to be on the ground. For the most part, your bush plants will be fine on their own. Tomatoes tend to be the exception and often need support even when growing in bush form.

Bush plants won't grow as high as a vine, so a stake or cage that is 2 or 3 feet high is often enough. To support an entire row of plants, put up a length of upright chicken wire as long as the row. Secure with stakes, and your plants can be tied to that instead of getting their own individual supports. Bush plants won't naturally grab anything, leaving you to tie them up to stay put.

Don't Forget the Fruit: This is one small extra thing to consider. If you have plants that produce really large fruits, like melons, cucumbers or tomatoes, you might have to get them some extra special support. When the plant is upright on a trellis, large fruits can break their stems and fall even before they are ripe.

TIP

Adding a small sling of **soft fabric can keep your fruit secure** while it finishes growing up on its trellis.

Level ③

Green Thumb

Natural Fertilizers

TIP

If you know a farmer, feel free to take any manure he wants to get rid of as long as you don't dump it fresh on your plants.

Natural Fertilizers

Fertilizer doesn't have to come in a box or jug with chemical warning labels on it. There are many ways to naturally fertilize your garden for added nutrients in your soil. In fact, by choosing a few choice ingredients, you can really fine-tune the nutrient levels to suit your plants better than you would with some broad-spectrum chemical treatment.

To keep things simple, a good dose of aged manure or compost is always an excellent choice for any garden. Stick with that unless you have some specific deficiencies you have to fix up. Mix in a load of it in the spring, and add additional compost about halfway through the growing season around the bases of your plants.

Now for more ingredient-specific fertilizing, do a soil test to see what you need and then get some of the following:

Extra nitrogen: coffee grounds, fish emulsion, bone or blood meal

Extra potassium: potash, wood ash, banana peels

Extra phosphorus: fish emulsion

Extra calcium: lime, dolomite or crushed egg shells

Extra magnesium: Epsom salts (the gardening kind, not bath salts)

Don't forget to take into consideration what you're planting. Not all plants need the same things, so don't treat your entire garden area as one big plot of soil. Low on potassium? Well, some plants may prefer that, so don't add any fertilizer to their beds and boost it just where it's needed.

As mentioned just above, if you are using manure for fertilizer, you need to make sure it is at least 3 months old. It needs to be aged or the very high levels of nitrogen still in the material will kill your plants.

Heirloom vs. Hybrid

This is another terminology tip that will almost certainly come up when you are shopping for seeds, especially in these times of GMOs and other manipulated foods. There can be a lot of confusion about heirloom and hybrid, so you should have your facts straight before you make purchases based on misinformation.

Heirloom: Think of these as the good old-fashioned seeds that your grandparents would have had. There are no strange cross-breeds, and you can be assured that any seed you save from these plants will produce exactly the same variety as the original plant. Many people prefer these seeds because they are more natural and are better options if you want to save your seeds from one season to the next.

Hybrid: Now, don't confuse these with genetically modified seeds. Hybrids are the result of natural cross-breeding, though it's done in a carefully controlled manner. You'll find hybrids if you are looking for certain qualities not usually present in the original plants. Varieties that mature very quickly, or are more frost tolerant, or produce dwarf-sized plants are a few examples.

The catch with hybrid plants is that the seeds they produce usually contain the features from one of the original parent plants, not the hybrid itself that you planted and grew. So if you collected the seeds from your hybrid plant, and grew them the next year, the results would be closer to the parents of your hybrid.

GMOs: While we're on the subject, here's a word about the infamous GMO. These are genetically modified organisms that are artificially created with gene manipulation, which is not the same as natural cross-breeding whatsoever. In most cases, the inserted genes don't even belong to the same species as the original plant. Long-term testing on the safety of these products hasn't been done, not to mention the possible damage to the ecosystem once their pollen and seeds start spreading outside their designated farms.

Heirloom vs. Hybrid

You don't need to worry if you are looking at a packet of hybrid seed. **It's not the same as the GMOs in the news.** Go for heirloom if you are collecting seeds at the end of the season.

Row or Not to Row

Row or Not to Row

The old-fashioned long row isn't your only option. There's certainly nothing wrong with planting in rows, just don't limit yourself to it.

Rows work great if you plan on using machinery in your garden, like a rototiller, and need the empty spaces for the wheels. Originally, tractors would have used the rows. If you're not going to use any machines like that, there may be little need to go with the row approach.

The problem is that a lot of space is actually wasted with all those empty rows in between your plants. Having a single long row of a single species of plant also makes pollination less effective. Long rows do allow you more walking space and easier access to reach from plant to plant during chores and harvest time.

These days, more and more people are trying the "square foot gardening" method instead. It's better for smaller gardens that don't need wheel routes. Your plants are organized in a quilt-like pattern of squares, with your walking paths between groups of squares. For example, one square foot block might hold an array of 16 radishes, or a single head of cauliflower. Check online for measurements for whatever you're planting.

By using this technique (or something similar), you cut down on all the wasted space between the rows, but you can still easily reach into each grouping of squares to do your chores. It also keeps your plants nice and close for more effective pollination. And that means more produce! Weeds between the plants are kept to a minimum with a good layer of mulch, so you don't need to worry about getting your hoe in between the closely placed plants.

TIP

Do a bit of reading before you decide on a layout.
It might sound complicated and too geometrical for your liking until you see some examples of how to plan your grid.

Rotate Your Crops

When you're new to gardening, it can be a relief to see your plants thrive and produce a great harvest. Once you've found the right blend of soil and sun exposure, you can be reluctant to tamper with a good thing. You'll have to be brave and embrace the idea of moving your crops around or you may regret it as the years pass.

For example, if you plant broccoli in the same patch, season after season, all the broccoli-loving pests are going to learn about it. The soil will be filled with eggs and cocoons from all the various bugs that like eating broccoli. They thrive on your plants each year, and then the cycle continues. The same situation goes for the mix of bacteria, molds and fungi that go unseen in the soil. The deck is stacked against you and your poor plants after a few seasons. This is why you rotate.

There are lots of different approaches, but the simplest is a 4-year plan. Each patch of your garden should have its occupants shift through 4 stages, one each year:

1. **Leafy** - spinach, kale, chard, lettuce
2. **Fruit** - literal fruits, as well as pumpkins, peppers, tomatoes
3. **Legumes** - beans, peas
4. **Roots** - carrots, beets, turnips, onions

The specific order isn't important, just that you keep things moving from one type of plant to the next. Allowing for at least 2 years before bringing the same kind of plant back into any one spot is going to help reduce your pest load, but 4 years is ideal if you can manage it.

A rotation plan can be helpful as long as you aren't spoiling other good conditions to make it work. Just do your best to make the rotation principle work for your garden area.

TIP

If you have a spot that is just **the right level of shade for lettuce,** don't try to make sun-loving peppers happy there.

Rotate Your Crops

Successive Sowing

If you are drawing out a grid or map to organize your garden space, **remember that you need to account for changes** as the seasons shift and time passes.

Successive Sowing

We're talking about organizing and planning again. This time, it's not so much about space as it is about time. To make the most of your garden, you want to use every inch but also every day of your growing season.

In practice, it means you plant seeds at many points through the season, not just all at once in the spring. Second and third plantings can help you make the most of your time.

For one example, you could plant a patch of radishes in the early spring. They'll be ready to pull and harvest in a month or so. Without planning ahead, their space would just sit empty now for the rest of the summer. If it's shady, you could actually keep planting more radishes if you wanted. Otherwise, it's perfect to plant something that prefers the warmer temperatures. Maybe some beans.

Later in the summer, when your main crops are finished, go back to thinking about your spring plants. They'll be just as happy in the cooler fall weather as they are in the spring. So if you have a month or so left before winter, revisit some lettuce or maybe even early peas.

Another aspect of successive sowing is deliberately planting certain crops in delayed batches so that you don't end up with one huge harvest at once. So if you need 3 rows of green beans for your family, do one row, wait a week before planting the second row, then wait another week to put in the last one. As long as you're not delaying anything past your frost dates, it should be fine. That means you'll have a more gradual load of beans to deal with later on.

Get International

This is a tip about thinking outside your regional food box. It's too easy to get into a rut about growing what is normal for your area, and leaving it at that. Now if you're lucky enough to live in a lush warm climate, where you can grow anything your heart desires, you might not feel the need to broaden those horizons. But for those of us living with more limitations, you can start to get creative.

Bok choy, lentils, and kiwi fruit may not be your usual garden fare, but they would be a fun and healthy addition to the usual North American line-up. We tend to make assumptions that "foreign foods" are also tropical, and that's definitely not the case.

To use those mentioned above as examples, you can grow the New Zealand-native kiwi even in the colder climates you'd find in Michigan's Upper Peninsula area. Just look for the hardy or super-hardy varieties, and they'll survive bitterly cold winters. Lentils are a Mediterranean legume, yet grows splendidly all throughout the USA and even Canada.

Never even heard of bok choy? It's a Chinese green that is somewhat like chard that produces green leaves and a celery-like stem. Versatile and delicious, it can give some great variety to your choice of garden greens. It will grow in the USA between Zones 4 and 7. Ever pass a kohlrabi in the store and wonder what it tastes like? It's a very strange-looking vegetable that seems to be a cross between a turnip and possibly an octopus. It's actually easy to grow and will produce a huge bulb for you in a fairly small space.

So whether it's about exploring plants that you wouldn't expect to grow in your climate, or just experimenting with foods from other cuisines, never limit your garden choices to the usual.

TIP

If you are going to try some exotic new foods, purchase a few from the grocery store first.
It would be a real shame to grow something you don't like to eat.

Get International

Adding Shade

Draping a light fabric cover over your plants is another option, though you can run the risk of overheating your plants this way.

Adding Shade

Though most plants thrive in as much sun as you can give them, you can have too much of a good thing sometimes. Get to know your shade-loving plants and give them the care they need.

Some examples of shady plants:

- Most greens, like lettuce, chard or spinach
- Some herbs, like oregano, parsley, mint or chives
- Peas
- Garlic
- Radishes

When it comes to shade-loving plants, the best scenario is a few hours of solid sunshine, and then light to heavy shade for the rest of the day. Being in shade all day is acceptable as long as it's not too deep.

Understand though that there is a difference between plants that can tolerate shade, and those that truly need it. Plants like cabbage, broccoli, green beans, turnips and beets will all grow pretty well in the shade if they must, but will be better in the sun if you can manage it.

With plants that do better in the shade, you should plan your garden accordingly. If you naturally have a spot on your garden that gets a large dose of shade through the day, that's the spot for the lettuce or mint. If not, you'll have to get shady on your own.

An upright piece of garden lattice works great to create light shade, as long as it's secured in place. Something like that is prone to blow away in a strong wind otherwise. You can also make a more moveable shade cover with a picnic table umbrella and stand. For a more natural approach, arrange your shade plants next to something that grows tall, like pole beans. Once your beans are high enough, you'll have some all-natural shade. A few decorative shrubs would also do the trick for this.

Edible Flowers

We've done a lot of talking about fruits, vegetables and herbs, but there are even more ways you can grow food in the garden. Have you given any thought to edible flowers? Granted, they're more of a garnish than a main-dish sort of food. Even so, you can bring new color and flavor to your meals with a few carefully chosen flowers.

Nasturtium: These pretty flowers are often found in various shades of orange or red, and they're one of the most commonly grown food flowers. Both the leaves and blossoms are edible with a very lovely peppery flavor.

Violets and pansies: The petals from either of these plants are just slightly sweet.

Calendula: In the marigold family, the petals of calendula also have a peppery flavor like the nasturtiums.

Daylilies: These large colorful flowers have a light "vegetable" flavor, some say it is like raw zucchini.

Petunia: Even this common flower garden resident is edible. The petals don't have too much flavor though.

Sunflowers: For harvesting, you should leave the flowers on the stalk until they are quite dead and starting to dry. Cover with a bag if necessary to keep the birds from snacking. You can let it dry completely indoors once the flower is dead. Eat the seeds raw or roasted.

Many herbs: Though not really grown for their flowers, many herbs do produce lovely blooms toward the end of their growing season. The large purple puff-ball blooms of the chive plant are a good example. The flowers are usually just as flavorful as the leaves, so go ahead and use them.

Another benefit for growing edible flowers is that you can grow "food" without anybody realizing it. Even just a few of these could make a little vegetable patch look like a flower garden.

Edible Flowers

Some neighborhoods or planned communities have regulations
about having food plants in front yards.
If you are forced to grow decorative plants only, these should do the trick nicely.

Think of the Bees

Make your garden a nice place for bees
by limiting your insecticide use.
Choose the most natural repellents you can,
and don't apply them during pollination season.

Think of the Bees

We've all seen the current issue with declining bee popula-tions all over the world. Without getting into this problem on a global scale, you do want to remember the bees in your own yard when it comes to planning out your garden.

Primarily, you want them around to help keep everything pollinated. Not all of your plants need bee pollination to make produce for you, but many do (think tomatoes, peppers, pumpkins and squash, beans and just about every kind of fruit). By planting a few species of flowers that are really attractive to bees, you'll help draw these helpful insects into your yard.

Plant These for the Bees:

- Coneflower
- Lavender
- Bee balm
- Catnip
- Primrose
- Cosmos
- Asters

These flowers are all lovely and have great scents. Having a few patches of these plants will attract bees, and give them a regular source of nectar. This means a very potent reason to keep coming back to your yard. As your vegetable plants mature and need some bees, you'll be good to go.

There are a few other bee-friendly tricks you can try around your garden to help with your pollination and to lend a hand to worldwide bee populations. For the crafty types, try building a bee house. Yes, it's a real thing. Solitary bees and mason bees are two species that are great fpollinators, but don't live in a traditional colony or hive like honey bees do. Bee houses are sort of like bird houses, except filled with small holes for the bees. Check online for plans and ideas.

Keeping a complete honeybee colony is a really big step. If you prefer, get in touch with someone who already keeps bees and ask them to keep one of their hives in your garden.

Dealing with Animal Pests

Insects are a big problem with any garden, but don't forget the bigger pests. All sorts of animals are going to look at your garden like it's a spread out buffet, and they can quickly do a lot of damage because of their larger size.

A fence is a possibility, though many common garden pests will just hop or climb over it. A four-foot fence would keep out most rabbits, but squirrels or racoons would just climb over. It would also keep out any roaming cats and dogs that might be happy to dig around and make a mess (it's unlikely they would eat anything). For deer, it would need to be at least 8 feet high.

You can kick it up a notch with electrical fencing if you really need to keep the animals out. Even just two or three lines of wire can be enough. One shock and most animals (even stubborn racoons) will be deterred. It's a little more technical than a standard chicken wire fence, and the cost will be a bit higher too. You can get the materials at large gardening or farm supply stores. Ask the staff for some tips on putting it all together.

Is fencing impractical for your garden? You do have other options. Animals use their sense of smell much more than we do, and you can repel many animals by adding a few less appealing scents to your garden. Garlic cloves, slivers of scented soap, puree of hot pepper, mothballs or even predator animal urine (you can buy this last one) can all work to make your garden less interesting to animals. You'll have to reapply many of these scents after a rain though.

What about underground pests? Gophers, ground hogs or voles can chew through a lot of roots and you will never see a thing. Obviously, typical fences won't help. With a bit more effort, you can install a barrier of underground fencing at least two feet down to block most burrowing animals. Just dig a ditch around the garden, add fencing material and then refill. Scent repellents can be a bit of a help if you can find some access to their tunnels. Otherwise, you may have to resort to poisoning or traps.

Not all animal pests are the four-legged kind either. Birds can be a real problem with some crops, particularly berries or any patch with new seeds in the ground. A sheet or two of light bird netting over your plants should keep them out.

Dealing with Animal Pests

Get Kids Involved

TIP

Getting a new generation interested in growing food is the best gift you give to the planet!

Get Kids Involved

You can help the environment by creating a new generation of people who love to garden and who understand what it means to produce their own food naturally. If your interest in gardening goes beyond your own yard, this tip is something to consider.

Let Them Help: This is the most obvious, and the easiest way to get your kids into gardening. Let them give you a hand with the chores. Keep it age-appropriate and don't risk any truly valuable seedlings. Kids can help pick weeds or even collect bugs. Planting seeds is always fun, as is giving everything a drink with a watering can.

Give Them Their Own Garden: A step further might be to give your kids a section of the garden all to themselves. Let them plant easy-to-care-for seeds and give them the responsibility of keeping them healthy (at least alive) and hopefully they can have some pride later when they pick food they grew on their own. They might need a little help, but try to let them take care of things on their own.

Kid-Friendly Tools: For either of these two approaches, you should have a few tools that are scaled down for easy kid handling. Many garden stores carry smaller tools that are actually sturdy enough for real use, but even plastic toys are better than nothing. It lets a kid feel truly in charge of their tasks when the tools are their own.

Serve Foods They Like: Kids aren't going to develop a strong love of the garden if they hate to eat everything you harvest. Keep your recipes creative and encourage them to try new foods while not forcing them to eat anything they really don't like. As long as they are enjoying the food you grow, they'll want to be more involved. Snack on raw veggies as much as you can, the crunch is usually a favorite with kids over the cooked versions.

Saving Seeds

Growing your own fruits and vegetables isn't only a healthy choice, it can be a really economical one as well. With a little luck, you can bring in bushels of food for only the cost of a few packets of seeds. What if you could even eliminate that cost? Saving your own seed each year can close that self-sufficiency cycle and allow you to have a more efficient garden plan.

By deliberately choosing seeds from the plants that do really well, you're going to continually be breeding plants that perfectly suit your garden. You can't get that kind of quality from any seed catalog.

Some plants are simple to save seed from. You just have to make sure the fruits are all fully ripe before you start collecting. Peas and beans just need some pods left on the plant until they are dry, then you just shell for the seeds.

Not all plants are that straight-forward, though. Root vegetables are often harvested before the plant goes to flower and seed. Same goes for many leafy greens. In these cases, you'll have to intentionally leave a few plants un-harvested at the end of the season, so that they can produce their seeds for you.

For even more complications, some plants take two years to complete their own life cycle (known as biennials) rather than the usual one. A common example is the carrot. If you want to save carrot seed, you need to grow a few plants and let them die back naturally after the first season. Leave them alone, and they will re-sprout the next year and produce their second year form, which will finally lead to flowers and seeds.

Label and store your seeds in a cool, dark place away from excess moisture and the threat of insect pests.

SEEDS

Saving Seeds

TIP

Label your containers with the kinds seeds as well as the date. After a couple of years, they will start to get old and should be used immediately.

85

Level ④

Garden Pro

Get Started in the Fall

Remember that the fall isn't only good for cleaning up.
It can be a time to get something started in the garden.

Get Started in the Fall

That's right, you can get some of your gardening chores started in the fall rather than having to wait all the way until spring.

There are two main reasons why you should get these plants going in the fall. One is to help move some of your planting chores out of the spring season. You have tons to do in the spring, so why not get a few things done early? The other reason is that it gives your plants that early advantage to naturally sprout the minute the temperature is just right for you. That's usually earlier than you'd be out planting.

So what can you plant? If you're into grains, winter wheat is one you should be sowing in the fall (the chapter on grains can fill you in more). Garlic is a more typical garden vegetable that can also be done at the end of the season. Just plant a clove about 2 inches deep, with the pointed end facing up.

You can also plant cool-weather plants, like kale or collards, late in the fall as well. If you plant them too early, they can actually germinate and start sprouting before the snow hits, which isn't want you want. You need the seeds to overwinter and wait until spring, so get them in the ground before the ground freezes, but not much sooner.

Mark the spots where you have things planted so you don't accidentally dig them up when you're getting the garden ready for other seeds in the spring.

It's not just about planting, there are other things you can do in the fall to get a head start on your spring garden. Adding fertilizer and compost is one. After you've pulled all your fall plants, mix in your choice of manure, compost or other natural fertilizers. The material will stay in the soil and help get things humming first thing in the spring.

Cold Frames

A cold frame is kind of like a mini-greenhouse and it can be a fantastic tool to get your plants started early in the spring.

The frame is basically a box, about 2x4 feet and deep enough that your plants can grow comfortably without their leaves hitting the top (so maybe a foot or two?). Then you top with a sheet of glass. The usual approach is to have an old wood-framed window for the lid, in which case you just build the box to match the size. You can either just lift the lid on and off, or add a hinge.

You set your seedling pots inside the frame, and the glass traps the heat inside the box. So when the weather outside is otherwise too chilly for your plants, you have a sheltered and warm spot for them.

In fact, it can trap the heat so effectively, you may need to prop open the lid to let it vent a little bit. Just keep an eye on your plants and see if they start to wilt. Don't underestimate how much heat these boxes can generate.

You can also use this technique with planted seeds rather than pots; just leave the bottom of the frame open. Just set it up over the garden section you want to protect, and let the seeds grow with the added warmth. When they are large enough, just take the frame away.

Once the sun goes down at night, your frame and its contents will cool down. Cover it up with a blanket or a few bales of straw to help insulate that heat inside. Or just gather up your pots and bring them back into the house if you don't think they can handle the night chill.

TIP

Be aware of the temperature!
Even a little thermometer inside the box can let you know how warm it's getting.

Cold Frames

Raise Up Your Beds

TIP

If bending over is a big problem,
take your beds one step further and build them on legs.
It will make it easier to garden standing up.

Raise Up Your Beds

Using raised beds is a great technique if you are trying to get a garden going in poor soil, though the benefits of this idea apply no matter where you live.

You can build raised beds with a supply of simple lumber and a few basic tools. They are just large frames of wood, around 6 to 8 inches deep. Fill them up with good soil and compost, and you have a perfect place to start planting some seeds.

Besides the issue of poor soil, there are a few other things that a raised bed can do you for you. The first is keep out some pests. Airborne bugs are still a problem, but the raised walls of the bed do keep out soil pests to a degree (especially during the first year). Eventually, your boxes of soil will have just as many bugs in it as the regular dirt does, so it's not really a permanent fix. Even if you don't make a bottom for your boxes, voles and other small animals may not find your garden because they tend to stay just a few inches below the surface.

If you really have trouble with soil-living pests, you can even create a bottom for your beds to make these work more like really large containers. Otherwise, leave the bottom open so your plant roots can get into the ground below your layer of soil if they need to go that deep. Alternatively, line the bottom of your frame with chicken wire before putting in the soil. Roots can grow through it, and things like gophers are kept out. Small voles may still get through the wire. If they are your main pest, get smaller gauge wire material instead.

A raised bed will bring your soil surface up a little higher, making it easier on your back and knees to get weeds picked or produce gathered.

Preserving Your Harvest

If you're lucky enough to live in a warm climate where you can grow fresh produce all year long, then you may not have to worry about keeping your goods for later. But for the rest of us who can't grow through the cold winter, you can try your hand at preserving fruits and vegetables. You have several methods to choose from to keep your June peas ready to eat in January.

Root Cellar: This is the simplest method of food preservation, though you have to have the right conditions to make it work. A cold and humid area in your basement can work, providing it stays pretty constant in temperature and doesn't actually freeze. Under these conditions, you can keep boxes of carrots, potatoes, turnips, squash and apples. They can hold on to the freshness for months. It's limiting but is a technique that can help preserve your food with nearly no effort on your part, and it takes no power to keep running. Just check your stock every week or so, and use up anything that is starting to get soft.

Freezing: Next for ease comes freezing. In these modern days, it's one of the most popular ways of preserving fresh food from the garden. It's less work compared to canning, but you do have to keep the freezer running all the time and space is going to be limited.

To successfully freeze your produce, you have to get everything cleaned up and sliced or chopped the way you want it. Some foods can just be frozen in large zip seal bags, but they stay fresher over time if you blanch first. A quick dip in boiling water (just a few minutes) will kill many enzymes that lead to spoilage, but it doesn't actually cook your food. Dunk immediately in ice water, pat dry and you're ready to bag and freeze.

Canning: Canning is the most labor intensive way to save your food, but your finished jars can be stored anywhere and won't require any power usage to stay fresh. You'll need to get a book on canning to learn all the details as it's too lengthy to teach everything right here.

Preserving Your Harvest

TIP

Proper storage can help spread your food supply out
so you aren't eating the same thing for 3 weeks straight.

Using Row Covers

If you want to create shade,
use something upright
that doesn't actually cover up the plants too closely.

Using Row Covers

Though they tend to be called row covers, you certainly don't have to be growing your plants in rows for you to use them. It's a very light fabric cover you put over your plants, and they can be pretty helpful in certain circumstances. Check out the garden store, it's not hard to find.

There are a few different reasons why you might want to cover up your plants. You can use them to protect from frost, to add a little shade during really hot weather or to block any really problematic flying insect pests.

For Frost: In these cases, the actual fabric you use isn't too important. The idea is to cover your plants up at night to keep that killing frost from settling in. You can even use a light bedsheet if you have to. Just gently cover everything at night, and hope things warm up in the morning.

For Shade: A shade cover can help you keep your plants out of the sun for a few weeks so you can get your spring harvest in. You probably won't want to try and use this technique to grow shade-plants all summer long though. A row cover will also hold in the heat and your plants won't do too well over the entire season.

For Protection: This can be the trickiest idea because you usually leave the covers on for many weeks, and you have to keep your plants growing under there in the meantime. Because these covers may stay for most of the growing season, they need to be done right (no hastily tossed bedsheets, please). Proper row cover material will keep out the bugs but let in nearly all of the sunshine, as well as the rain. The material will also need to be held up with stakes or wire hoops so that it doesn't directly weigh down your growing plants. You'll have to make a point of lifting the ends up periodically to take a look at your plants, to check on their health.

For Heat: In this case, you'll want to use something like light plastic rather than the usual mesh fabric. Heat-loving plants like some peppers can benefit from some added warmth, just make sure they don't bake.

Pruning and Cutting Back

It can be really hard to start slicing and dicing at your plants, especially after months or even years of tender loving care. Rest assured, it really is the best thing for them (providing you are doing it right).

Cutting Back: A cluster of leaves heavily infested with mites, aphids or mildew is easier to just clip off rather than try to clean everything off of it. Dead branches can also be cut off to prevent further damage. Just don't overdo the cutting when you start to see yellowing leaves or dying branches.

Another aspect of cutting back is the pinching out of unwanted flowers, particularly at the end of the season. If your remaining growing time is short, you don't want plants wasting their precious resources on new flowers or new fruit that will never mature.

One last reason to cut would be to keep some plants from getting too tall. A plant can put a lot of energy into creating new runners and adding new height. If you are looking for more fruit, snip off the top couple of inches of the vine.

Pruning: The easiest place to start with pruning is to remove any dead branches. You aren't too likely to hurt the tree, and removing them can help let more light into the tree. It also lessens and chance of damage when the dead pieces break off (they eventually will). From there, you can move up to taking out any smaller branches from the interior of the tree. It allows more sun into the center of the tree, which will help more fruit develop. Better pollination, too. Anything more complicated should be shown to you by a professional.

Pruning and Cutting Back

Use Your Greywater

Use Your Greywater

G reywater is the "technical" term for waste water coming from your home, such as washing machine rinse water or the water going down the drain after you do the dishes. On the other hand, black-water is the term for the more serious waste (think toilet). Blackwater isn't much use, but you can take advantage of the many, many gallons of greywater your home is putting out.

This tip is more about conserving limited water supplies rather than providing a better water source for your plants. Greywater will have various soaps and other contaminants in it, and you'll have to make a few changes in your daily routines to take advantage of this water source.

To reuse dishwater, the simplest idea would be to have a dishpan in the sink so you can lift out your water when you're done. Toss it out onto your plants, and you're done. A handy person might adjust the pipes under the sink so that you can drain out into a bucket. The water can go right into the garden, or poured into a larger barrel to be distributed later.

Washing machine water is a little tougher though it does represent a much larger volume to work with. You need to do some plumbing work and have your machine drain out into a barrel or cistern rather than out through the home's sewage system.

You can even reclaim your bath or shower water, though it can be a little tougher. Again, a little plumbing rework or extra buckets can do the trick.

In any case, you need to keep your chemical use to a minimum. That means natural or otherwise environmentally-friendly soaps need to be used. If you've been washing anything toxic or unpleasant (like a really greasy cooking pot, or washing clothes stained with paint), then you should avoid using that greywater.

TIP

Many people who garden in very dry climates can reclaim a great deal of *FREE* water for their thirsty plants with greywater.

Microgreens and Sprouting

The term "sprouts" tends to make us think of healthy-eating hippies in the 1970s, but the trend is actually still going strong today. We just call them "microgreens" instead. The idea is that new little seedlings are extremely nutritious as the plant is undergoing all its germination processes. So you let your seeds get started, then harvest soon after for tasty and healthy green on a small scale.

Older sprouting would only let the seeds undergo a very short period of growth, barely getting their roots out. Today's microgreens are left to grow a little longer to produce a few leaves along with the roots.

This is a great gardening option for anyone who is really tight on space or is impatient to have some fresh food on the table right away.

Microgreen Techniques: Use shallow pots or seedling trays, filled with loose potting soil. Plant your seeds (see below for some ideas), and keep the soil moist. Lighting isn't too important for most seeds since they are under the soil anyway.

Once they start to sprout, keep them near a window or under a light. You'll be harvesting before the plants fully develop so it's not all that crucial to provide perfect conditions. As much light as you can is best though. Let your little plants keep growing at least until they have their first set of true leaves. You can leave them until there are 2 or 3 leaf pairs out there. Then just use a pair of scissors to snip them all off at soil level. It only takes 7 to 10 days, and you can have many handfuls of fresh greens ready to eat.

Leave the roots to break down in the pots, and plant another round. If you prefer, you can pull up the plants and enjoy the tender roots along with your microgreens. It just means a little extra washing before you eat.

What Can You Grow? You want to focus on quick sprouting and fast growing plants that have edible leaves from the start. Here are some of the more popular choices:

- Beets
- Arugula
- Radish
- Kale
- Cabbage
- Chard

Radish sprouts are quite peppery in flavor but the others are a lot like mild greens that may slightly taste like their more mature counterparts. Use them like you would any other fresh greens.

Microgreens and Sprouting

Sprouting is a fun project during the winter when you don't have enough space or light to garden in the house.

Companion Planting

Do your research, not all plants go together!
Dill and carrots, beets and pole beans, and cucumbers and potatoes
are all bad companion pairs for the garden.

Companion Planting

As you ponder your garden space, trying to figure out what should go where, you should take one further thing into account: companion planting. The general idea is that some plants just go really well together.

We already mentioned how you can pair up tall plants with shade-loving plants when arranging your garden's space. There are a few other well-known match-ups you should know about. Though not all companions are the same, the usual scenario is that one plant either repels or attracts insects to help protect another. It's natural and effortless insect control.

Here are a few examples of plant partnerships you can try:

Tomatoes and Cabbage: The aroma of the tomato leaves will repel some of the worst cabbage pests, like the caterpillar of the diamondback moth.

Basil and Tomatoes: In this case, the basil actually improves the flavor of the tomato's fruit. It's not always about pests.

Carrots and Rosemary: Rosemary keeps away the carrot fly.

Corn and Pole beans: This is a very old-fashioned companion tip, with the sturdy corn stalks creating a natural trellis for the beans.

Green beans and Potatoes: The green beans will help keep away several species of potato beetle.

Marigold and anything: Marigold blossoms deter a large number of beetle species and will work as a general pest repellent anywhere.

Get Cooking

Making the most of your garden isn't only about what you grow, it's about how you use it. Without some skills in the kitchen, you'll be using your harvest for nothing but salad and that isn't going to go very far in giving you food independence. The more dishes you can make with your vegetables, the more you can benefit from your garden.

Take a class or two at your local college or community center, or find a gourmet-minded relative to give you a few pointers. Even just some basic skills can open up whole new worlds of vegetable cooking. Browse around the many recipe sites online and see what photos catch your eye on Pinterest. Don't be afraid to experiment a bit.

Worried that you just don't have time to cook more? Get a slow-cooker (also called a crock pot), and you can make all sorts of home-cooked meals by tossing in your ingredients in the morning, and serving up a hot meal at the end of the day. You can also learn about "freezer cooking" where you make a few dishes all at once, and freeze them for later. That's another great time-saver.

Vegetables don't have to be relegated to side dishes all the time either. Move them to center stage to make them more of each meal. A thick vegetarian lasagna or a hearty pot of bean chili are a couple quick examples.

Even baking can get into the act, and not just your fruit either. Shredded zucchini and carrot go fabulously in muffins with dozens of recipes out there to choose from. You can always use another way to use up that zucchini.

You have tons of fresh produce coming in, so don't be afraid to use it.

TIP

Not everything can come from the garden.
For cooking, make sure the pantry is stocked
with spices, sugar, flour, and other common recipe ingredients.

Get Cooking

Level ⑤

Frequent Farmer

Growing Mushrooms

If your mushrooms don't look like the species you had in mind, **throw them out.** They may have picked up some wild spores and **may not be safe to eat.**

Growing Mushrooms

Not for the gardening novice, mushrooms can be a difficult food to grow. Still, you can produce great crops of them with a little patience and attention to detail. They actually can make a fun indoor growing project if you want to experiment with something different.

What You Need: You're going to need a box of "substrate", or possibly even a log from a particular kind of tree. That will depend on the species of mushrooms you want to grow. A typical box of material might be straw, sawdust, shredded newspaper or aged manure. This will be your garden space.

A dark location that you can control the temperature is your next requirement. It will need to be warm, so a basement may not be suitable. Closets work very well as long as there is space to safely add a heater.

Next, you need mushroom seeds, or fine microscopic spores. They come imbedded in wooden plugs called spawn. Find them online or in a specialty store, most gardening stores won't have them.

How to Grow Mushrooms: Fill up a box with about 12 inches of your substrate material and keep it damp. Press your spawn into the material. If you are growing mushrooms that need a wood substrate, you may need to drill holes in a log to hold the spawn plugs. Keep it in the dark, usually at a temperature around 7OF to get things germinating. Check it out after a few weeks. Fine downy fibers should start spreading out from your spawn plugs. Your mushrooms have begun.

Drop the temperature down to 55F, and let them keep growing. You just need to keep the substrate damp and the lights off. There shouldn't be any problems with insect pests, or any of the other usual issues with garden plants. Just watch the emerging mushrooms. They should look reasonably like the species you want, especially after a few weeks. If they look very different, dump the whole batch at that point and start over.

When your mushrooms are nice and mature, gently pluck them to harvest. If you leave the network of fibers undisturbed under the substrate, they will continue to produce more mushrooms for you.

Growing Grains

G rains can be a tricky crop that requires more space than the usual vegetables and many home gardeners don't get involved. If you've got the room and really want to grow some staple crops for your pantry, keep reading.

Wheat or Oats: These are the two most commonly used grains in the house, and would be a good place to start.

The usual variety of winter wheat is sown in the fall, and it comes up very early with the spring warming. Oats are usually planted in the early spring, and you want to get hull-less oats for easier processing later. The growing process is basically the same for both crops.

Neither are not planted in rows, but rather just tossed out over your loose soil. Give it all a rake to get the seeds covered with a thin layer of dirt. At the end of the season, you slice off the seed heads as the kernels are just ripening and can be slightly dented with a fingernail. Spread out all the stalks indoors where they can finish drying completely, and then you have to get threshing. The seeds have to be broken loose from the seed heads.

A simple method is to lay out a large sheet, cover with your dried stalks, cover with another sheet, then stomp all over it to break up the seed heads. Next comes the winnowing, or the separating of your grains from the unwanted stalk bits. The old-fashioned way is to get out on a windy day, and drop big handfuls of the material from a few feet above the sheet. The wind blows away the chaff and your wheat or oats collect on the sheet. You can make do with a strong fan if the weather won't oblige.

After all your hard work, you can expect around 8 bushels of grain from a quarter acre of garden (that's for either wheat or oats). While a quarter acre is a lot of space for some people, that really is a good bounty. Use as-is in all kinds of cooking, or get a grain mill and make up your own flour.

Growing Grains

TIP

Do a little research into rye, barley, buckwheat spelt **OR** millet for even more options. **Rice is a difficult plant to grow** for the home gardener, so don't count on that one.

Getting into Trees

Cooler areas can easily grow apples, cherries and walnuts, **OR** you can get into the whole citrus family if your winters stay above freezing.

Getting into Trees

Trees can be a little daunting, but they can be a big boost to your garden production without much extra work. You can get many kinds of fruit from trees as well as nuts or even tap for sap and syrup. For the moment, we'll stick to the fruit and nut harvesting.

The two biggest drawbacks to a tree are the space they need and the time investment. Typical plants will produce something for you in the first growing season. You'll have to be more patient with trees. It's fairly normal to wait 3 to 5 years (or longer) before you get anything from your trees. If you're fine with that, then you'll want to address the space issue.

You'll usually have 2 choices when buying trees: standard or dwarf. If you're tight on space, go for the dwarf. A standard apple tree, for example, will require at least 10 feet of space around the tree, though you can plant other small plants closer than that, you need to have at least that much room for the crown of the tree. But for that space sacrifice, you can get around 10 bushels of apples from a single tree each year. That's a lot of fruit! A dwarf tree will require about half the space, and produce about half the harvest.

Fruit and nut trees are usually purchased as saplings, rather than started from seed. An older sapling means less waiting time before you get any fruit but it will be more awkward to transport and plant a bigger tree. When you plant, dig a hole about twice the size of the existing ball of roots, set in the tree, and fill in the space with good loose soil and maybe some compost. Spring is the best time to get a tree planted.

Once your trees start fruiting, you can expect to bring in the bounty for at least a decade or more. A good walnut tree can give you nuts for up to 50 years.

Keeping a tree healthy is a little different than your usual vegetable plants. Occasional spraying may be necessary to keep the insects at bay, though there are many natural options for that. You'll also need to learn a bit about pruning. Cutting away dead branches is the simplest approach, and you can also help your tree with some further strategic cutting.

Get Into Grafting

G rafting is about taking living pieces from one plant, and attaching it to another plant where it continues to grow. It's a technique used in growing fruit trees mostly, and it could lead to some interesting experiments if you have space for trees in your garden.

Why Graft?: The general reason is that you want to combine aspects of two trees together into one. Each section keeps its own qualities though. They don't really "blend" together.

The most common reason to graft is to create dwarf fruit trees. Using the root portion of a naturally dwarf tree, you can replace the top with another type of fruiting tree, and the resulting tree stays dwarf in size. That means you can turn any tree into a more manageable size without having to actually breed a new dwarf variety.

One interesting benefit of grafting is that you can create your own unique tree that may produce several kinds of fruit, which is a huge boon to anyone trying to raise food in a small space. Some impressive grafters have created huge trees that can produce dozens of different kinds of fruit.

Lastly, it means you can take advantage of a really successful tree you already have. You could harvest some fruit and seed, and hope that the offspring trees are just as great. But you're taking a genetic gamble. On the other hand, you could take a few branches and graft them to other root stock, basically created clones of your original tree.

How to Do It: To simply add a grafted branch to an existing tree, you need to cut a careful notch in the base tree. Then trim the end of the branch to snugly fit. Insert the new branch, and tie the whole thing tightly together. Grafting wax can help seal the wound until the tree heals over on its own. The new piece will immediately start to draw water and nutrients through the open tissue, but it will keep its own unique genetic qualities. With a few seasons of growth, you can hope to see flowers and fruit on your new branch.

Get into Grafting

When grafting different kinds of fruit,
keep the trees closely related.
Varieties of apples will work together,
or even oranges and lemons on one tree.

Harvesting

TIP

Double-check anything you forage
AND have a good plant guide
handy to identify harmful plants.

Harvesting

Believe it or not, you can get more food from your yard than what your garden produces. In fact, you can pull in a decent edible harvest with no garden at all, if you have the right environment and know what to look for. Edible plants grow all over the place, and you can forage for bushels of food and never spend a moment actually "gardening."

Here are some wild food plants that you can get started with:

Dandelions: Let's start with the one plant you are guaranteed to find somewhere nearby. The leaves are very edible though the young, small leaves are going to be the softest ones. Those could be eaten raw but the older leaves should be cooked like any other leafy green vegetable.

Plantain: Another very common lawn weed with wide leaves and tall spike flowers. Again, the leaves are quite edible with the smaller ones being better for raw salad eating.

Lamb's Quarters: Also known by the less appetizing name of pig weed or goosefoot, this is yet another tasty green you can gather up from most yards. The leaves have a slightly whitish cast to them and have a distinctive tooth pattern along the edges.

Wild Garlic: Though you can't see the familiar underground bulb, you can often smell that unique aroma when you're near wild garlic. They look like cultivated garlic, just smaller. Look for those long grass-like leaves in wooded areas, and use your nose.

You can gather baskets of these extremely nutritious greens that cost you nothing and just need to be picked. Make sure the plants haven't been sprayed with pesticides.

Sell Your Surplus

This is a tip to help your garden make more of a positive impact on your life, and possibly the lives of the people around you. Having an income from all your hard work isn't too bed either. But if you look at it from a non-monetary point of view, having extra produce to sell helps bring natural, possibly organic, and locally-grown food to more people. So where do you start?

The simplest way to sell your extra produce is to do a little networking with friends, co-workers and neighbors. Make up a few packages of whatever is currently fresh and keep it priced reasonably. You just sell when you have extra, or when someone asks about your garden.

If you want to step it up a bit, you can always think about getting a table or stall at the local farmers market or flea market. There will likely be a cost for your table, a set schedule to follow, and you'll typically be surrounded by other people selling much of the same stuff as you. Still, it can be a great way to make some sales and find like-minded people who are interested in locally-grown food.

Selling from a table at the road is another option but it can be tricky, depending on your location and neighborhood traffic patterns. You don't get the same audience as a market does, but you're also not bound by anyone's rules. You can open any day you want, and skip days when you're busy or have nothing to sell. It's also free.

Another method currently gaining popularity in the gardening world is the CSA. It stands for community sponsored agriculture. The idea is that you sell shares in your harvest before your growing season starts. This allows your customers to better support your garden, because you're paid early to help with seed and fertilizer costs. After that, you portion out everything you grow to your shareholders. They get ongoing produce based on whatever is growing well that year, and you get upfront funds. It's a little more complicated than the other methods but might work for your situation.

Sell Your Surplus

Think About Chickens

TIP

Rural areas or small towns generally
have no problems with backyard chickens,
but check with local regulations if you're a city dweller.

Think About Chickens

Not for the average gardener, but if you have a large enough yard and live in an area that allows a few chickens, you might want to consider starting up a small flock.

Why Keep Chickens? Actually, there are several reasons why a few hens makes a great compliment to a vegetable garden. They are great for insect control, though you might not want to let them free roam around your garden too much. Chickens do eat some green plants and will scratch up new seedlings.

Their used bedding is fantastic for compost. Unlike horse or cow manure, you don't need to let it age. Just shovel out the old straw and mix it in among your plants. Very rich in nutrients, and it won't cost you a cent.

Lastly, it's about adding to your food-production goals. You're already growing fruit and vegetables, so why not produce home-raised eggs too? Technically, you can also get meat from your chickens, but the average gardener isn't up for that kind of processing. Eggs are easy to collect, and will be continually produced by your chickens for years.

Actually Doing It: All the ins and outs of keeping chickens are a little too much to completely outline here, though it's not as difficult as you might think.

You'll need a secure little house that is large enough for your chickens, along with a nest box or two and a roost. Add straw or wood chips for bedding. Fence off a part of your yard so they can safely explore. Feed your chickens a proper feed from an agricultural store, not just kitchen scraps. Make sure to give them clean water as well.

Once your chickens are almost a year old, you'll start to get eggs. You don't need a rooster. An average chicken will lay an egg once every 2 to 3 days. Check frequently so they don't go bad outside.

Bonus

⊘ TO GROW⊘

Leeks, Scallions, Spring Onions, & Fennel

 1. Use the white root end of a vegetable that you've already cut.

 2. Place the white root end in a glass with a little water and place in a sunny place like a kitchen window.

 3. The green part of the vegetable will grow, just cut it off when you need some for cooking. The remaining white root will keep producing.

⊘ TO GROW⊘

Lemongrass

 2. Once it starts sprouting, transplant it into a pot and place outside.

 1. After cutting off what you need, place the root in a glass jar and near a sunny window.

 **3.** Wait until the stalks are about a foot tall then cut whatever you need, the plant will still grow.

**Celery, Bok Choi,
Romaine Lettuce, & Cabbage**

 1. Similar to leeks, these veggie re-grow when their white root is placed in water.

 2. For these, however, place it in a shallow water—only enough to cover the roots.

3. Place it in a sunny window and lightly spray the top part of the cutting with water so it doesn't get dry. You can also plant them into the soil, but keep it very moist early on.

Ginger

2. The smallest buds should face upward. Place it in a window with indirect sunlight.

 1. If you have a spare piece of ginger rhizome (the thick part you cook with), plant it in potting soil.

3. It will grow on its own, and once it's large enough, harvest and cut off another rhizome for your next plant.

TO GROW
Potatoes

1. If you have a leftover potato that is growing "eyes" (little bumps that look like they're sprouting), cut it into 2-inch pieces.

2. Leave the cut pieces to sit at room temperature for a day or two to dry.

3. Plant the pieces 8 inches deep in nutrient-rich soil. Only cover it with 4 inches of soil.

Add more soil as roots appear.

TO GROW
Garlic

1. Regrow the plant with a single clove. Plant it root-end down in soil with direct sunlight.

2. Once the plant produces shoots, cut them a little so the plant will focus on creating its bulb.

3. When you have a new bulb, use it for cooking and re-planting.

Onions

1. Cut off the root end of the onion and leave half an inch of an onion on the roots.

2. Plant it in a sunny spot with moist soil. If it's cold outside, move your pots indoors.

3. When you have full-grown onions, keep replanting the root ends.

Pineapples

1.  Remove the green leafy top and make sure all the fruit is removed (it will rot and kill the plant if you don't).

3.

2. Slice small, horizontal pieces from the bottom of the crown until you see root buds—small circles on the flat base of the stalk.

Remove the bottom few layers of leaves. Plant your pineapple crown in a warm environment. Water regularly, then only once a week once the plant is growing. It won't get to your plate for 2-3 years, but you'll have home-grown fruit.

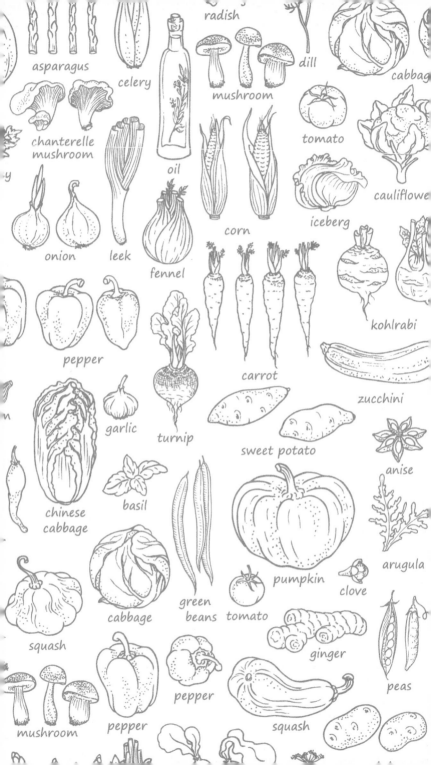

"Square Foot Gardening" by Mel Bartholomew, Rodale Press, 1981

"Lois Hole's Vegetable Favorites" by Lois Hole, Lone Pine Publishing, 1993

"Vegetable Gardener's Bible" by Edward Smith, Storey Publishing, 2009

"Organic Gardener's Handbook of Natural Pest and Disease Control" edited by Fern Marshall Bradley, Rodale Books, 2010

Author Bio

Terri Paajanen has been living on 5 acres for the past seven years, growing a wide mix of fruit, vegetables, herbs and even a few apple trees in her gardens. Before that, she worked hard to produce food in various small city lots, containers and balconies. Over the years, she's honed her backyard agriculture skills and learned the tricks to a successful garden without the heavy use of chemicals or synthetic products. Terri has a B.Sc in biology and botany and has mastered the fine art of putting bushels of food on the table every year. She is looking to expand her home's acreage and plans to experiment with nut trees, more fruit and joining a new farmer's market. Terri is also the author of FIG's 52 Simple Ways to Live Green published in 2014.